*Sometimes We're All Living
in a Foreign Country*

Books by Rebecca Morgan Frank

The Spokes of Venus
Little Murders Everywhere

Sometimes We're All Living
in a Foreign Country

Rebecca Morgan Frank

Carnegie Mellon University Press
Pittsburgh 2017

Acknowledgments

I am grateful to the editors of the following magazines in which the following poems have first appeared, sometimes in earlier versions:

Connotation Press: "Leda, After," "Gunning for It," and "Crusoe Is Still There"; *Crab Orchard Review*: "Evolution"; *Cream City Review*: "The Movements of Mechanical Objects"; *Crazyhorse*: "Fishing Tackle and Fine Wine" and "Pilgrimage"; *Diode*: "Extinction" and "Eastbound"; *The Gulf Stream: Poems of the Gulf Coast*: "Crawfish Chorus," "The Whole Town," and "Postscript from Mississippi"; *Harpur Palate*: the first section of "Rosewood Triptych"; *Hearth*: "The House Is the Cause"; *International Poetry Review*: "Pawn Shop"; *I 70 Review*: "Parable of a Firstborn," "April," "The Welty Tour," "Revitalization" and "The Soloist"; *Mead*: "Love Song"; *Missouri Review Online*: "The Causeway"; *New South*: "Night Halos"; *The New Yorker*: "At Sea"; *The Paris American*: "Out of the Ruins"; *Poetry South*: "The Book of Bells, Chimes, and Carillon" and "Pyre"; *Reunion: The Dallas Review*: "Bird's Eye"; *Sidelines*: "The Ivory Gate" and "Piney Woods"; *Southern Indiana Review*: "The Mothers," "How to Be Reckless," "Rubbernecker"; *Sou'wester*: "The Bridge"; *Switchback*: "Manuals for Trains"; *Washington Square*: "Jesus & Tomatoes"

"The Moon's Magnetic Field Once Came from an Asteroid" appeared in the anthology *Even the Daybreak-35 Years of Salmon Poetry*. "Crawfish Chorus" was reprinted in the anthology *The Manifesto Project*. "Pilgrimage" was reprinted in *Verse Daily*.

This book was completed with the support of a Mississippi Arts Commission Artist Fellowship and residencies from the Virginia Center for the Creative Arts and the CATWALK Institute. Thanks to my students and colleagues at the University of Southern Mississippi, and to my friends, near and far, whose kindnesses and conversations carried me through this book. A special thanks to poets Jessica Murray, Phoebe Reeves, Hadara Bar-Nadav, and Megan Grumbling; photographer Betty Press; and my Mississippi writing partners, Allison Abra and Alexandra Valint. Thanks to the wonderful folks at Carnegie Mellon University Press: Gerald Costanzo, Connie Amoroso, and Cynthia Lamb. And to my husband, John Warrick, partner in all things.

Book design: Bronwyn Kuehler

Library of Congress Control Number 2017937498
ISBN 978-0-88748-625-8

10 9 8 7 6 5 4 3 2 1

for my mother, Jane Frank
1942 – 2016

In the life of each of us, I said to myself, there is a place
remote and islanded, and given to endless regret or secret
happiness; we are each the uncompanioned hermit and
recluse of an hour or a day; we understand our fellows of
the cell to whatever age of history they may belong.

—Sarah Orne Jewett

Contents

I.

II.

I.

Pawn Shop

I'm seated at the boxy and floral pianoforte,
surrounded by shoestrings, an old leg bone,
a cracked Grecian urn. I'm face to face
with a child mannequin in ruffles, a gyrating
mini hula dancer for the dashboard,
a silver gravy boat, a bottled seascape.
There's a globe spackled with globules of color,
and someone has tried to scratch off Alaska,
to turn it back into the base blue, still water.
I'll finish the work: glue on the china bear
figurine, free the sailboat from the bottle
and send it afloat on uncharted waters, punch
the inflatable clown if he gets in my way.
Before I leave this place I'll buy it all back—
A gun. A violin. Someone else's puzzle.

Parable of a Firstborn

I never left the yard, I never took
   a single drop of blood
or let the dog out the fence to die.

Only once did I take my sister's hand
   and lead her across six lanes
while she covered her ears to the horns' sea,

and even then we sang jump rope
   rhymes and rocked our heels
by the side of the road: *catch a tiger*

catch a tiger, catch a tiger by his toes.
   I filled her milk-stained bottles
with water, cooked noodles and hot dogs,

let her put catsup on her toast.
   She barely ever cried.
We kept away from the hole in the wall,

kept our shoes on when grandpa
   died. I never once, not once
told a lie. But we'd sing and chant

Hoppity, hoppity, hoppity, bees
   how many rabbits
like to eat cheese? Everything we knew

was in the big fat books: a 1950's
   Britannica, the *Better*
Homes cookbook, the one with the tabs.

The picture bible that got lost in the basement
        or yard. She won't tell it
like me, you see—she'll find an angled blame.

Ever since she crossed the river and knew
        what we hadn't seen,
she's like someone who found the blindfold

and ripped it off and can never forgive
        the joke. Everything good—roller
skates, the tabby cat—she won't tell you

any part of that. Once, I saw her in the super-
        market aisle. She harbored a giant
catsup bottle, a baby in her cart. I saw

her face crying up at the lights. The mother
        looked right through me.
Hard to say who lived last, lived first.

Crawfish Chorus

Crawfish, crawfish,
Mary caught a dogfish.
Dog face, dog race,
send her down the Brown's place.

One, two, three, the roof's
done broke free: now
the water comes and
lifts us all up.
You are not it.

And the wind whirls round
and lifts us up.
And the wind rolls round
and puts us down.
Lightning strikes twice.

If you reach right in,
a catfish.
If you reach right in
a catfish.
Will swallow your arm
and spit you back out.
Swallow it, chase it, chase it
down with a coupla crawfish.
Craw. Craw. Craw. Fish.
Crawling. Fish.

The Whole Town

Ripe wrack and ruin, that's not a life.
The strife of a swallow, black-
shelled along the bottom. Sand me
down to the grit shoal, wait.
I can open. I can stretch my jaw
like an alligator and move
the whole town through this
swamp. Easy. I was born below
these trees. I saw the birds seed
and die, the water move through
like a train. The highway melted
down and made new moss.
I waited and waited for the rounds,
the swing up. But that's for
the bees. They never once
got swept out to the Sargasso Sea.

Manuals for Trains

I was born with a train in my ear, its pitched
blast invading my body like a tuba-parasite.

Each conductor has a signature move.
I fell in love with the throating of the 3 a.m.—

his consecutive wails warp my dreams
and choke them into new directions.

On holidays, I can't sleep, wait
for the schedule, long for the surprise

of delay, a new man at the helm making
his mark on my landscape without ever

leaving a footprint. Not once seeing
my face in sleep even though I conjure

each him, how he feels in the power of speed
breaking the black with fierce bursts.

I am an echo chamber for passengers
headed somewhere else.

They never stop for me, never open
their doors, just power

through these crossroads without
even a wave to my waiting.

Love Song

You're a tin can tied to a string. A green bean. A rattle
        on my caged bird. A blue ventriloquist to your songs,
your long mourning. You sleep on it. Wake it.

        I am minute and a minuet. The footwork is simple: I
could pass for a shuffle, a soft-shoe, I
        turn and bow, I go through the motions. I float.

You're a boastful note, the hand on the waist—
        There's a landscape you belong in, leaked paint
past the page. You're an autumn lake. Glistening.

        I am august. I am a chain link fence, chain mail,
a chainsaw working its way through the legs of your table,
        your deck, the tree that leans over you when you read.

We're a rock face. A defaced fence with a split for crawling
        through. We're a blueberry patch left for a past
that lasts. We lick our fingers. Before longing, it's winter.

The Mothers

It is supposed to come naturally.
The way you loved a boy whose father held
a gun in his own mouth, as his mother
shouted, *grab it and run!* And the gun cracked
against the creek rocks, then washed away.
If I had a baby, I would hold it close, erase
the cuts that severed us. I would spoon
it stories and know my love was guzzled
whole, to be spit into the future like a bottle
hurdled across the lot. Something to be
excavated, examined. Every blizzard buries
something we've left, or worse: what we never
had. The white ash of love is no different.
Listen, I say, and the baby nods. Sleep,
and I'll tell you another one.

April

The fixed month, the month of rain.
Like the packed snow it left behind,

or the split in the forgiving tip that bursts.
The light lifts so slowly, it could still be dropped.

Breath on the white dusted ground.
A kind of solitude. Ditched here,

his eyes whitening like a newborn, milky
with love and nothing. But I've been

longer than a week. I am constantly still.
I watch his groping about the world.

The field of light-dust caught in burrs.
Like gum to the shoe, like words to the throat.

Jesus & Tomatoes

My uncle says the stigmata came from an accident in the kitchen.
The way my cousin would hold the disfigured in his palms and
quarter them right there, dumping the salt in the center. The way
he'd suck them out as he cupped his bowl, his greasy hair hanging
around it like a shroud. The way he was careless with the ax, the
bicycle, the refrigerator door. The dull knife slipped from a thick-
skinned heirloom. The boy don't pay attention, my uncle said, and
I didn't dare ask him how he'd cut both palms, whether the salt
burned in the wounds. I always set my tomatoes on the chopping
block after that, mitted my hands and took the sharpest knife. I
wash my hair twice each morning, move breakable items as carefully
as if they were lungs waiting to be transplanted. Anything to keep
from dying. Anything from having to be born again.

How to Be Reckless

Small town life closes in on you like a pigsty gate.
You want to climb over it and go drink in the barn.
To feel something in your blood or on your skin.
A pinch lets you know you're alive. And then you
need more. You're running barefoot in the mall,
swiping coins from the fountains. Splashing.
You start to sing in the aisles, toss the books across
the library and café. You limbo under the police tape.
Jump over the bar and pull the most expensive
bottle to your lips. Steal a taste from a stranger's plate,
then bite his wife on the neck. You kidnap a neighbor's
kitten and feed it to the wolves. Stick your arms
down a gator's throat. Kiss the checkout clerk for giving
you correct change. Shoplift kiwis and juggle them
on top of someone's Mary Kay car in the lot.
You steal a trombone and bugle it up at the top
of the water tower. You jump from roof to roof.
Line up all the pills and count them, then blow them
into the air and stomp. Sit down at the bar's piano
and knock out the first part of "The Entertainer." Look
someone in the eye. Admit when it's time to leave.

Nobody Is Sleeping in the Sky

title after Lorca

A straw slices through a telephone pole
like truth in a long marriage.

Once the house was blown over to its side.

We used a ladder to climb up
and drop ourselves down in the front door.

The roof was lifted off and landed just a centimeter
over.

The drapes were sucked to the outside of the house;
to draw them, you hung yourself out the window.

As silent as the answering machine still in place,
the house around it gone, the tiny tape sucked out.

Afterward, you opened the front door and
every window blew out.

A tree stripped bare, a chicken plucked clean.

Then, our bodies touched even in sleep, even below
the mattress that held us to earth with its weight.

Rubbernecker

The flaneur does not know what to do. His city
has been lifted up and scrambled. The favorite

brasserie has had its eyes smashed. Walking
paths bear fallen trees and debris from missing

houses. *Where have I put it, my pocket watch,
my passport, my Costco card?* This is a Midwestern

flaneur. He wears cowboy boots and has given
up smoking for his health. He walks by workers

bearing chainsaws and boxing sandwiches. Across
the way, a pastor surveys the smashed grandiosity

of his now steeple-less vessel. Even a flaneur whispers,
god bless, and hopes the gods of godlessness

understand. Traffic is stalled everywhere. It seems
it's best not to leave one's home. But what can

a flaneur do? He steps over live wires. Finds
himself wanting a lens. He thought he'd seen

everything. But disaster asks too much of him.
He's done looking. Lies down in the ditch, which

saved a man there the day before. If you hide from
these vast forces, sometimes they spare you.

Gunning for It

Have you ever held the cold power
in your palm? Have you seen the warmth
wiped out of skin? Either way, you know
the numbers are gunning for you. They'll track
you down anywhere with ease. Violence rests
everywhere, unearthed histories. Take me,
for example: an ancestor shot a man in the head
once—he stopped a mass murderer
in his tracks. How do you explain a history
like that? By telling the whole story? How
he once left another man for dead,
having hit him over the head with rage?
The innocent man happened to live, just
as the guilty man died before taking lives.
Justice just an accident where violence
meets its match, lucks into the victory of merit.
You touch the gun, it breathes in, breathes out.
Plots a future of its own, weighs its chances
of righteousness, of the right hand unwavering.

The Welty Tour

In the next room, Peter's gloved hands crack
cordoned-off spines: he has been granted
permission, his agent's call his pedigree.
So the tour itself is only the docent and me.
He is docile, eager to please, leads me
up the stairs and takes me to the bed.
The coverlet is authentic, he says.
He lectures me on the heating system, offers
an anecdote of a broken casserole, recites
all of the Welty lore he has rehearsed.
She taught him when he was young, and now
he serves her legend, lets me lean in
toward the books—I cross the line
of what's allowed, never touching.
He shows me photos—two loves lost, one
a married man—then on the way down,
pauses before a feather in a box,
reciting Yeats's "Leda and the Swan."
He begins to weep at *Let her drop*, adds,
Like Welty's loves! Now I stop—
is he comparing her to the god, or Leda?
He cannot bear her, her Unfulfilled Love.
I cannot bear this either—how dare he conjure up
for her such disappointment, such wasted longing?
I want to be the mirror of her photographs,
to be her figure of my own conjuring. I want
to believe I, too, could be happy here, in this
solitary house, in this small town, amidst
the rows and stacks of books. Untouched.

The Movements of Mechanical Objects

Someone keeps opening the music box
in the middle of the night.

It used to play "Clair de lune," now
plays Muzak versions of the latest pop song.

I sleep with one eye open.
The figurine has surely been pushing

her way out. Her toes are so slender
she can pry open the lock.

Her sleek limbs bunch their muscles
as she lifts the lid, and

for seconds, she looks
like a sumo wrestler in her tutu.

If you asked her, she'd tell you
what it's like to be buried alive.

To spin on command.
She's been studying to be a DJ.

There are lots of classes on the internet,
she'll say. A girl can be anything.

But the dark trope only lets
her rise into a sea of pink

with plush dolphins.
Maybe I'll grow up,

she says, looking around,
to be a veterinarian.

You don't tell her that her veneer
is wrinkling and her belly

bulges like a squeezed tube.
Her eyes chip

away without her notice.
It won't be long until

she's retired. The body
junked and thrown

from the box. Separated
from everything that moves.

Sometimes We're All Living in a Foreign Country

Only the older woman at the tire store asked
to know my name—she worried about finding
me a husband. In the abandoned downtown,
I rattled the window cages and called out,
looking for life. I visited the nearby
taxidermist and considered being preserved
as I was, joining the ranks of raccoons
and squirrels. Out at the mall, life milled
around like schools of fish. On the highway,
the engines roared like everywhere else.
I thought I knew a little about small southern towns—
what it meant to leave to live.
Now every direction takes me to a foreign land.
Every turn returns me to a history that's my own.

The Causeway

My mother used to tremble every time
we crossed the Potomac, the Delaware, every
river on the road North. Her body tightening
into a steel beam, as if it alone could hold
the bridge in place, the car afloat. She taught me
never to trust what was underneath you, to drive
right toward the liquor store near the motel, where
she'd melt the steel back to liquid, to watery
sleep. Every trip a chance to die again across
a bridge, and every breeze a threat. Even now,
I hate the feel of a ceiling fan, an open window,
anything that might blow me off course. Still,
my body turns to statue at this majestic gesture
of two roads across the water, the light glistening
to let me know I've left behind the closed doors
and am headed toward a city of life—I stay my course.
I imagine strongmen from the circus holding each
pylon in place and the fish swimming below me
whispering and feathering out knowing that they
have nothing to be afraid of anymore.
I want no part of their world, nor they, mine.

Crusoe Is Still There

All the trees have left me.
They left behind the birds.
The birds left, and left
behind their songs.
I keep singing them
here, in the desert
of my loneliness.
Sometimes I see
flight far above
in the atmosphere.
Astronauts, honeymooners,
a flock of something
quick and passing.
I wonder if they look down.
I wonder if they see
me and think *I didn't
know there was life
down there.* I wonder
if they hear my song.

The Moon's Magnetic Field
Once Came from an Asteroid

When you walked in
it was like recognizing

the moon when he returns.
His lover bites his cheek; she

has no choice. All we see
is the dissolution, then await

the reconstruction.
Each time, the sky

yanks her into his orbit.
I want to say *I'm sorry.*

I want to say
You win. Our bodies are like

the confessional booth these
poems are stuck in. Even

the priest can see that sin.
You'll be all spit and honey—

or maybe I'm the poisoned
flower gnawing on its own

lip because it has no hands
to reach for you. Only words

that are as useless as the pollen
for saying anything. I continue

to serve them even with your hands
around my throat from across

the room. Your voice is home,
I answer it like a bat guided

across the atmosphere. This
is a narrative that cannot end

well but wants to, but must.
I'll continue to go down kicking

and you'll be sweet as anything
until you bite back. No, it can't

end here—we won't let it.
Billions of years have passed

since an asteroid last hit
the moon: clearly some

magnetic fields can be sustained.

Piney Woods

It's been more than a hundred years told
since someone first discovered what a pine

could do. It took more than half
that time to realize the ways remnants of a tree

could kill: a forest and the preservation of its fells
could become something evil stripping the house.

They dug up the neighborhood across
the tracks, erased all traces of the pine,

what each forest had been cooked down to or
brined in. They said that all the bad ground

is locked up somewhere else, that I can breathe
easy on my evening strolls. But every time

I've tried to lock away what hurt me, it seeped
back up. The poison now within me, to stay.

Historic Preservation

When morning came I found
a catfish in my arms, writhing
with the weight and violence
of a sturdy man under attack.
I forgot to breathe, forgot
that all around me the water
was now oil. The stone walls were
covered in moss, but I could only see
the plaster, the flowered paper.
My chipped cup. Sounds broke
it all into pieces: a trill, a chatter.
No one else could hear them.
The whiskered burden grew still
in my arms. Not once had it looked
my way. I held it, I held it in
my arms, and watched it rot.

Bombed

in memory of Vernon Dahmer 1908 – 1966

Ellie's body broke through the glass like
    a gasp—she'd been fumbling with the latch
beating her shoulder against
    the pane
as the smoke bottled up between her and her little girl.

The fireball was born on the carpet, had roved
    like a drone, honing on the sleeping bodies
as bullets peppered the front rooms
    of their home. Her husband Vernon
fired back, burning.

From down on the ground she raised her arms—*Vernon!*
    he passed the dangling limbs: the youngest,
Bettie, who was only ten, shrieking from the burns.
    They were afraid she might die. A child
will howl fiercely when hunted in her own bed,
    flames feeding her first excruciating pain.

Ellie and Bettie hobbled to the barn, refugees from their own
    home. Vernon fending off the firing in the front, rooms
flaring alongside each trigger pull, the skin hanging
    from his arms. He soon followed his wife,
afraid the shooters would track his family out back.

Death came slowly, the pain of scorched skin. Vernon
    dead in the hospital by the next day's
end. The sons—soldiers, four of them—were safe.
    This war was at home in Hattiesburg,
Mississippi, where amidst the neighbors

. . . there were people mean enough and cruel enough they
wanted to kill me . . . the wonder
still laces Bettie's voice, nearly fifty years later.
They called themselves Christians, she says.
I was only ten. It was 1998 before Samuel Bowers
went to trial for that murder again.

Rosewood Triptych

There's one at every lost stop—
a place to dig up dropped coins, lost keys.

Some sort of archeology of movement,
a recorded passing through nowhere.

Something hatches in these places of waiting—
rootless tapping, the ghosts of valise,

hatbox, duffle—
conjunction of the last stop

and every platform ahead.
Memory is a cultivation.

The difference between not stopping and stop.
Bronze placard on the crumbling brick.

The was-a-stop, the yet-to-be-a-stop, or out there
an old caboose in an open field, rusting

roost for rodent, crow, lone man with a dog.

Nothing here but an old pole—
        no longer even a whistle-stop, no one
           to visit or leave.

Ruins of houses breathed in the wind
        through the cracks, generations
           of cats claimed

each home as a hatch, a half shell
        life of hunting, no more
           humans

who were themselves hunted, who hid
        in swamps, wading away
           from mobs.

The junction of lynching and arson
        bequeaths all civilization
           to the dandelions.

Bronze bells ring as the train creeps by
        without a hint of stop
           or wave.

Flight—

        during the last

whistle

    the railway car

        hatched

flights of moths

    flooding

   in
        conjunction, sunrise

a hapless cultivation

of bodies

bronze

   in the light.

Postscript from Mississippi

When you asked if it rained bees or poison
you were asking the wrong question. Again.

You still didn't understand the difference
between hurricanes and flooding. Thus between

gods and humans. Between your slum-
lordy digs and the shacks I pass that cling

to old boards and huddle around each family.
The yards marking the care of home.

Everywhere something is falling on
someone and I watch like an autumn

tourist tripping through the Berkshires.
I reach to catch a leaf. I try to straighten

a Pisa-like sapling. The wind wraps around
us both like a question mark and leaves

me standing, the sole witness on this end.
I'm telling you about a place of silence.

You want it all to be a metaphor. I'm watching
a front porch crumble. Still, someone sits there.

II.

Eastbound

We were on the eastbound train, passing clumps
of clapboard houses between butter-stick glazed
marshes with their shrubby populations, skeletons
deleaved, debirded: barren even now in the depth
of summer's sunset, and you were reading something
aloud about mammals, or maybe bats, and plucking
an imaginary bass in your lap, and the staggering populace
and stink made us a moving city, an urban damned
world moving over flats of water, noising
through towns. But you were not there: just me, sliding
along the blue seat wishing for you across the table,
you crooning one of those Irish tunes just for me.
You were back in your living room, the silent television
telling you things you cannot say, muted
characters speaking out your paranoia. But here
in the café car, the world moves quick and steady,
and I am not afraid. Not of your fist
punching the wall, your voice raised against
itself, your confessed worries that I'm married
or stealing your passwords or working for the CIA.
You pretend you're joking but the window is always
cracked for me to confess. I don't mind
the puffs that calm you, the tensions that move you
like a chill, the gaps when you stop mid-sentence as if
receiving an incoming message you're not sure
whether to attend to. I'll take out the bottles,
remember dog food, hold your shaking
body—but here's my world floating by
in a bubble, the one which presses its face to the glass
and calls me back to to-do lists, requirements,
social graces and all the familiar faces

of my accordion life, stretching and pulling
in contrast to your closed house and its secrets
and the way your eyes looked into mine to see
if I can be trusted or am undercover. Everything
about me a ruse. The sun is setting, and we
are riding on a train, but in reality you
are back in your yard watching the dog, and I
am watching the golden darkening fields, thinking
back to a picture of me in a yellow bathing suit:
I'm small and standing by the pond, waiting for you,
and I have no idea that one day you'll be waiting
for me, alone in your living room, doors locked,
shades pulled; instead, I'm running across grass,
arms open, running past your small self
lying in the yard sucking in your lips.
You're watching the world spin and splinter
itself into a million butterflies, drowning
in your first psychotic visions, and the sun sets
around the train windows and around your living
room and I'm still running and the seat's still
empty and I reach across to kiss you
chastely, to touch the air around your eyes. Think
I'll save you. I imagine you sit up and catch me
in your net, back when your imaginings were harmless
fancies, back before I hopped the train
and left you to your mercurial unravelings.

The Freedom Tunnel

After the train tunnel under Riverside Park where people made their homes in the '70s and '80s. They were evicted in the early '90s.

Jonah:

I'm in the belly of the belly.
Does it matter whose? Whether
leviathan, whale, some other
beast who savors flesh and mind.
This belly swallows cold metal, is
a body snaking between boroughs,
stretched deep down in this clump
of space garbage floating along through
pitch. Event horizon? That is Life.
Without, I am still only space.
With, I am an unnecessary part
of a beast that will swallow anything.
I don't even hear the trains anymore.

I live with tracks that wind,
vacant, below the city, full
of caverns and ledges, lean-tos
made in the pitch and damp.
There are guard dogs and camp stoves,
makeshift spigots and wiring
down from the above-world. A new
kind of upstairs/downstairs means
million dollar properties have
bowels below their basements.
Manholes are the elevators and
there's an alligator-attitude
to the decorating: swallow what
gets in your way. You're in the guts
of the beast, the teeth of the city

ready to consume you. I worked
Wall Street and then I worked
an alley in Chelsea before it got
hot. Now I live beneath. Here,
even God can't make his way
through the passages. They say
Amtrak has a map, will smoke us
out. I light the match to win. Peace
is to own by neglect and claim.

            Doc:

        I became a scientist because I wanted to see
        the midnight sun. I imagined a girls' chorus,
        a hallelujah, as if the archangels would lift
        me up from the top of the earth once my vigil
        had frozen the sun. To feel that light, the flight
        of everything. To float up like a balloon filled
        with someone else's breath. No longer bound
        by the darkness. And in the daylong night,
        the snow would turn despair to light, reflecting
        in its white streetlamps, windows, torches.
        I never made it up there. I still hear the voices:
        Come up here, to the top of the world—
        Toward the sun, toward the place where life
        continues in the marriage of day and night.

Jonah:

The weeds were wrapped around my head.
Why even try to remove what winds

around me like a serpent?
A plant can be carnivorous, proto-

or even borderline
carnivorous. What I mean to say

is anything
can devour you. Look around

the household. It will swallow you,
that detail of your life. So petty

and ravenous. I have never
had a taste for anything.

World, my chore. *The depth closed me*
round about. The depth closed me . . . .

Yes, the earthly bars. Yes, the bottoms
of the mountains. You've heard it all.

It's all in the book. How could that be
a God's to feel? The fingerprint

of human angst stamped
on every line. *Even to the soul.*

My only sin was to have been born—
my curse, all wit and no will

to love or praise.
I was a broker. I failed.

Doc:

Imagine yourself in an army of butterflies
stampeding a flower's castle. A war
of beauty. This is the mind. A series
of stations coordinating action. Even
an ant's ankle has a control room.
Now imagine an electric socket shooting
across the room. A ceiling blown off
in a tornado, a car crushed in a hurricane.
These forces at work, who controls
them? The world of the mind is also
so recklessly governed. We cannot expect
to control it. Each post of the mind linked
to one another. Each so easily blown
up, surged. But note: repair is possible.

Jonah:

You ask me if I'm lonely here? Send in
doctors, priests, energy healers, support

groups and Prozac. Sackcloth
and ashes. Sit.

Like a king. Like
a believer.

I was alone in the world.
I was alone in the ship's hold from which

I was yanked.
I am in a prison within

whichever prison you put me in.
Solitary my punishment. Ours.

We live down here because we can.
Because it contains us.

       Doc:

       I, too, was once as small as a sand flea.
       Mountains ranged above, buttercups towered:
       "Chin up!" And then I saw sculptures on the head
       of a pin. Someone had made them. Proved beauty
       could rest anywhere.
                 Look, there is life inside
       the depths, a million microbes. And in the sea,
       everything mirrored smaller and larger. To feel
       small is nothing. Our amphibian nature allows us
       to move in and out of the depths

it pushes us under. Crawl to the shore. Crawl
into the distance of everything we have made.
We are part of a much larger machine.

Loudspeaker gives one last call to clear the tunnels.

Jonah:

I am nothing without
your flesh. You held me,
every cell of ours
connected, a contraction of
your reaction. I was being swallowed
whole, no part of me
behind in the lone world.

The violence with which you
tried to push me out—
I prayed to the cells around me
to reach and hold me.

If you've ever entered a cavern
where the lights were clipped
you've had a taste
of true darkness.
There is nothing for the eyes
to be responsible for—there is always
an elsewhere.

There in nothing, I was
something. A disturbance,
but symbiotic.
When Whale breathes out,
Whale holds me close.
With nothing to contain me, I am
Nothing.

I will wait. Return. Rebuild.

Leda, After

I felt the needle go in.
I was in a swan body, I
was all down and feather
and puddles. Everywhere
I could hear myself calling.
I migrated away from my
Self. It was cold there.
Formations occurred
around me. The truth
is that the sound
of thousands of wings
flapping around you
is similar to a thousand
hooves of an army. From
the center you are bound
to be beaten, buried.
Even in air this can happen.
Even among your own.
Yet the current changed
and airborne I was
suddenly alone. All
clouds. The silence now
its own stampede.

The Ivory Gate

You contorted into a carved figure
knived by the mouth of gods.

Your side muscular, moving like
a horse, put down, drugs draining the rise.

Soon, the eyes of the lungs grew
heavy. I climbed beside you, untangled

the limbs, fingered strands of hair. Parted
your lips, afraid the air would forget

its way. You burned as if rocket-
fueled, pink-skinned. A proficient heart

even in a battered machine.
I could hear it working, dutiful

with its hammer. Counted each strike
as if I myself were a metronome. Until

you began to move. Your eyes
opening, the vision gone.

Evolution

The wings return into the bird to nail him.
                                        —*Paul Eluard*

The soul is housed in steel and screws,
a you that's forged and saved. The way you move
is shaped by unheard clicks and pops, these small
pieces of you floating in blood and tissue.
My hand on skin is also hand on hardware, the supple
and scented cover now one part of a couple:
the other half resists my gripping caress
probing for your industrial edge, crafted
for you before they sliced you through.
You are cyber, hollowed, say
it feels nothing like a phantom limb or a graft
from the dead. What's in you not human—you dream
of steel cells drifting up into your heart and
turning it into tin. Of hardened breasts and hands.
Wake and ask if I could love an industrial shape
that your soul filled like a racket of birds, moving
through the forged ribs, the hollow lips.

Out of the Ruins

Sometimes you see heads freed of their bodies
in museums—kept alive with eye sockets, ear wells,

lips the maker's hands once carved on marble.
But here these heads are faceless, attached to bodies

in death: the casts of Pompeii. In the rotted absence
of a body buried and bound in ash, a negative forms.

When filled with plaster, the body rises back up
as a replication that can be repeated. Still,

the void is the only maker. The figures wait
in a foggy gallery: hunched, fingers pressing

cloth to the blank where there would be a mouth,
trying to keep a volcano out. Sprawled, shackled.

Either way, there would be no escape—
the figure of the man echoes the dog who,

also chained, is on his back in the moment of death,
an act of supplication. Across the room (the city—

everywhere this is happening), a man reaches, still,
for his lover. Knowing one dies first.

Even then, in sure death, someone is left.

At Sea

Every few seconds, to recall captivity,
the mind slipping in on itself and its past,
and knowing it. She sounds like a politician:
I cannot recall. I am afraid I do not remember.
If only the mind could bury itself at the bottom
of the sea, wavering tentacles flexible
to the new currents. Instead it rides the rising
waves, bobbing up again and again,
drifting farther away from land it was not
meant for, from everything familiar.
And yet sometimes a detail will emerge, like a nose
pressed up against the aquarium glass,
the jellyfish trying to make sense of the nostrils,
the dim lighting, how it came to be, and be here.

The Soloist

She fights alone,
crouched like a lion
fixated on its prey,
her target invisible as
she fiercely battles
air, slicing and jabbing
against the beat
of the oversized drum,
all a part of this collection
of dances and choreographed
fights staged in the city park.

The others had worked
in pairs, but she works alone,
her eyes holding none
of the theatrics of her
predecessors, nor the peace
of the two youths she follows,
whose duet flowed
in balletic meditation,
their face lifted as if to a warm sun
on a slight autumn day, which this is,
September's perfection
which has brought us, curious
spectators, to this street fair.

We had all been happy
in our strolls, in our late
summer attire, in our casual
observation of what we stumbled
upon in our weekend leisure.

But we do not like her,
the way she works alone, knifing
the core of something
that creeps around the circle;
we do not like her, not
the giggling sorority girls,
the mother rocking the carriage,
the cop on his bicycle who
has stopped to stare, not me
standing alone in the crowd,
watching her punch out the lack, me
with my own knives, me with my chase,
as if I could beat down love itself,
and make it love me back.

The Book of Bells, Chimes, and Carillon

I wonder about the untouched skin of a bell.
The way it swings, dark-marked

by the hard slap, packed melodious
wallops strung against it, leaving scars.

I want to palm it like the inside of a mouth.
My touch will choke its sound or force a call.

The chimes hold nothing; they bump
and grind, find a way to move in air, even

when the hand, the instrument is not there.
The carillon is vermillion sound,

sets its stakes as the sum of its parts.
A warning serving as the city's conductor.

Together, the bells are rich and cold, their gold
grappling and crackles thunk across highways,

fields, a train yard and whistle.
They sing a loneliness the city longs from.

Close the covers. Cover our ears.

Revitalization

He twines his thumbs over the lone
apple tree's branches, feels downward,
fingers girdling over the gnarls
and scabs, like absent fists.
Once downtown was an orchard—
No one knows why this one survived.
Roots now threaded back into the earth
through a surgery, a careful dressing,
fungus removed from the base.
The buildings remain untouched,
fractured and peeled, surrounded
by ghostly rows clothed in mourning.
The whole orchard bows.

The House Is the Cause

The house is the cause of wind—
its job being to break it.
Absorbing the cold
through brick and plaster, through
blood. The house is a skin.
Knocked over, the contents
have no meaning.

In the woods I saw the tent. A heap,
a puddle. A pot with a spoon left
to gather. Now the wind is beating
at our doors. Where there was brick,
there is air, a tear. There was a smell
in those woods, like something long dead.
Like the flesh, letting in air. I was there.

What We Are Looking At

When the taxi driver told me what he'd seen
by the side of the freeway, I pictured a plastic

horse of my childhood, toppled, then tossed
out of a trailer, unable to find its legs. Like a cow

tipping gone wrong at an LA exit, drivers gaping by,
nearly causing a pile-up. But the truth was worse—

the horse tethered by its tail to a pole, bloody.
No one sure if she had been beaten or shot

until the expert says it was an accident, not abuse.
You see, she strangled herself, tried to get free

of the ropes in the trailer as it moved across
the asphalt, her legs in stillness behind the running

motor, her eyes fixed on the steel wall ahead.

The Bridge

When the bridge was strung over the water
it looked like Christmas, a temporary
lacing of stars connecting the banks.

When the first trucks crossed, the bridge
shook. Passengers quaked, imagined watery
deaths, calculated the odds of swimming
to shore and gasping in the mainland.

They imagined stocking their cars with pickaxes
and life vests, listened to sopranos sing
elegies on the long commutes.
Carpooled so as not to die alone.

They packed lunches to eat under
the surface, as if the car would be
a fishbowl, with water snakes wrapped around
the glass, turtles looking in. Imagined
imagination was the best defense.

For a death one envisioned was impossible.
But soon they dreamed of crossing to chase wind
turbines or to rest under a canopy of live oaks.
They dreamed of arriving in a city that evolved
into a carnival at night, lights beckoning.

Fishing Tackle and Fine Wine

That's the sort of city it was. You could find
everything you wouldn't want within a block.
Bloodworms, feathered flies, a Bordeaux
that would put you back a week or two on bills.
The corner market carried charcoal for the yards
no one had, and the rats were disgusted
with the takeout restaurant's scraps. You had to
wear your flip-flops in the shower and your coat
in the bed. The sidewalks went from salt to dry dust
that the fan stirred around when it wasn't
missing a beat. We'd stretch out in the median
and slurp popsicles in psychedelic shades, watch
the pretty girls in flowered dresses ride by
on bicycles, baskets full. We wanted
the coolness of their circling limbs,
the loose ponytails easing across bare skin.
We watched the cars and wished for wings, cold
things, the pond on the far side of town.
We didn't talk about how you'd drowned, or
the way we both missed your skin, your lips,
red, then orange, then purple and cold.

Extinction

We were tied to the weather.
Outside, houses turned their backs to the wind.
The dead sipped what was left from the ground.
The snow cover turned stale, darkened.
There was nothing left to discuss.

We were game heads, stares fixed,
tongues thick and permanent
in my molded gape, your grimace.
We couldn't taste anything.
The carpet beetles were eating us alive.

Pyre

He folded me into a paper boat and launched
me down the Charles River. Lit the match

and tossed it into my origami mast, watched me
burst into my journey. Drowning and ashing

in every breath, I held on to the letters stamped
across me. The ink doused the ignition, but words

buoyed me along. I hung from the vowels
like a monkey in an artificial jungle, swinging

as if there were somewhere to jump off
to. From the shore, my dead girlfriends

waved, as if to beckon me into their ranks.
I was all crease and fold. They hadn't aged a bit.

I dove down to the bottom of the river
where the city's history had sunk into itself,

and the fish stared back at my intrusion.
Grief didn't belong anywhere, but I wore it

like an outraged barnacle bursting from my skin
like I was some grotesque creature made immortal.

Night Halos

This is where the dead still dream.
From the North, the ice, as if a steel
halo dropped from constellations, lights
the latch, frozen shut, but easily cracked.

You can see the sky through the worn patch.
The brick throat breathing past the bodies in blankets.
They stare in silence,
each tucked in separate walls.

Luck has seasoned the beams and broke them,
and even these posts forgot their making.
He tends the goats and caulks the gaps.
He harvests tree sap, blueberries, branches.
The green has passed. She sleeps.

They walk on dried petals, seeds, bones.
Everything dry in their mouths.
It's always the longest month of the year.
They sink, hot weight in the well.
Become what swims back up and gasps.

Flight Patterns

begin in a wooden box—a queen, three pounds
bees, a coffee can
of sugar water all tossed from bin to bin,

then trucked over hot pavement, flung as freight
on to the plane. A frost
can take the whole crowd or leave

a small buzzing alone amidst the bodies.
More than an inch of corpses
should be refused—no money-back

guarantee. No burials, no issues of disposal.
But bees can survive
up to ten days, can make it from me

to you in half the time we will spend apart.
I'll send them ahead,
ask them to make you honey, something

sweet to nourish you. Any dead bodies
collateral of correspondence,
a sign of what is left unsaid

in absence. The sting a way to feel something
without a body there.
Open the package with care—the weather

here is cold today. We missed you enough
to die en route,
to lay our bodies before you.

Pilgrimage

The clouds went through them like a ghost.
They left no chill.

They took something and sailed it across
the range. Peak to peak.

Then farm and further in to village,
the shrubs of suburbia, the city, the sea.

No one noticed the pilfering,
bodies still moving, empty, back on the ridge.

A man marched up with a golf club,
a girl raced the ridge in barefoot shoes.

Quarreling couples with packs leaned on metal poles.
The rocks crumbled. More clouds moved

through the rising crowds. No one
noticed that anything was missing: a memory,

a yearning, a taste, a tendency to whistle.
A fib, a family secret, unwritten tunes.

The magpie clouds were dark in light skies,
whitewashed in blues,

and they built their nests
with what they took from inside.

The people on the ridge parked their cars
and jingled and joked their way up.

Felt strangely lighter on descent. Left
laced with the smell of mint and pine and mud.

Later they would check their shoes, feel
a pebble that wouldn't reveal itself, a nudging—

something so gone it couldn't be noticed.
The littleness of theft.

The magpie clouds spilled their wares
and possessions washed to shore.

Stuck in sand to a foot, were drunk in salt.
This is how the earth continues to weigh the same.

We lose a fear, a memory of the dead.
Grow a longing. A reach.

A whole body ache.
Swallow the clouds as they swallow us.

Bird's Eye

Even the littlest surface molts,
a fragile striptease.

The skin of the forest first—
tanked contraptions smoothing miles.

Then old stations and theaters rot
from the inside.

Glass offices glisten, shatter.
Ranch houses fall like dominoes.

New layers scab over the artifacts
and blemishes.

From the distance, everything remains
the same. A blue-green wash.

A marbled cloud cover.
A rusted-out galaxy corner,

set in the dreamer's mind across light,
across flesh, skeleton.

From a distance, there are no bodies.